LANKYBOX

THIS BOOK BELONGS TO

....

THANK YOU FOR BEING OUR VALUED CUSTOMER. WE WOULD BE GRATEFUL

IF YOU SHARED THIS HAPPY EXPERIENCE ON AMAZON.

THIS HELPS US TO CONTINUE PROVIDING GREAT PRODUCTS, AND

HELPS POTENTIAL BUYERS TO MAKE CONFIDENT DECISIONS

COLOR TEST PAGE

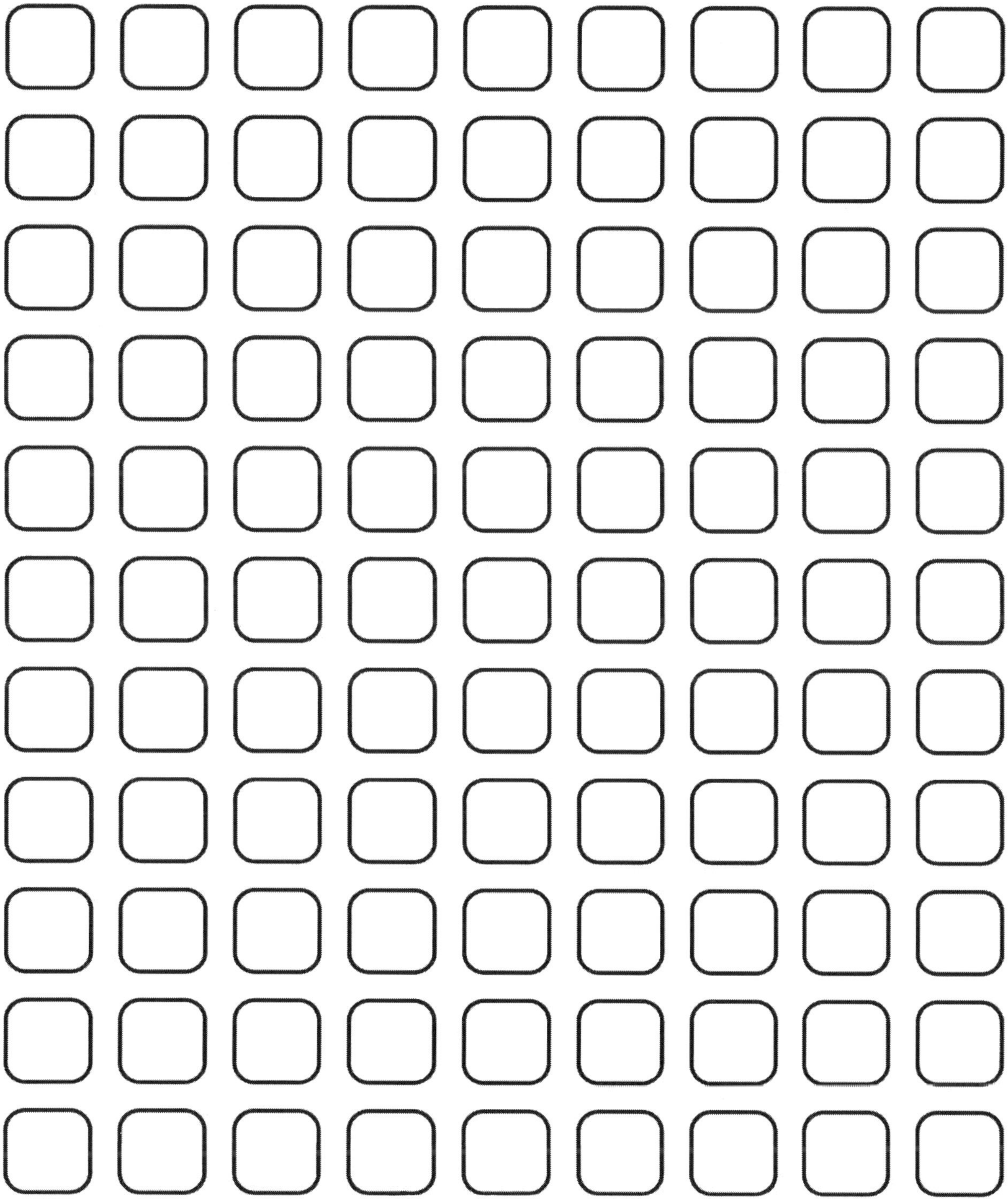

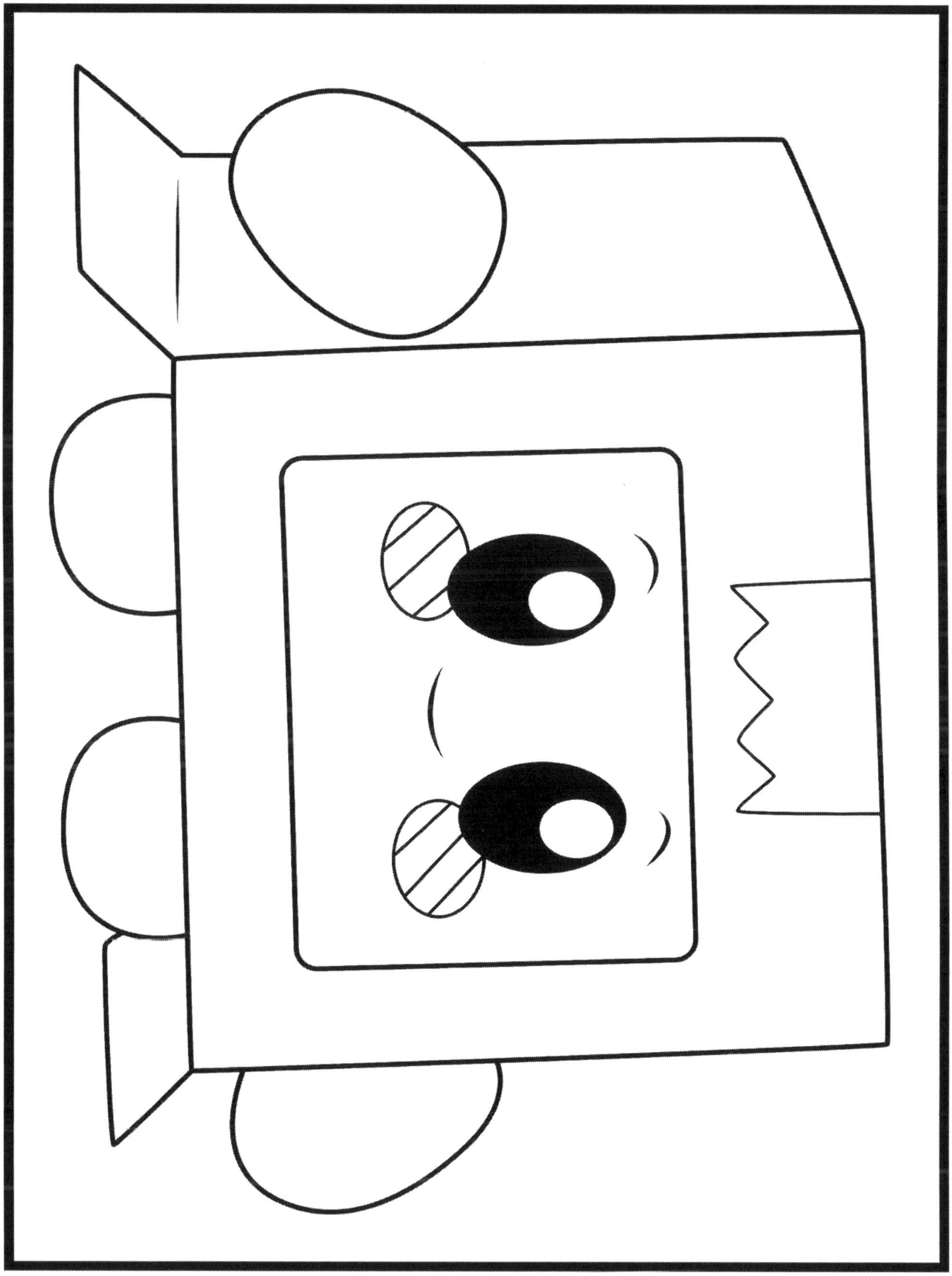

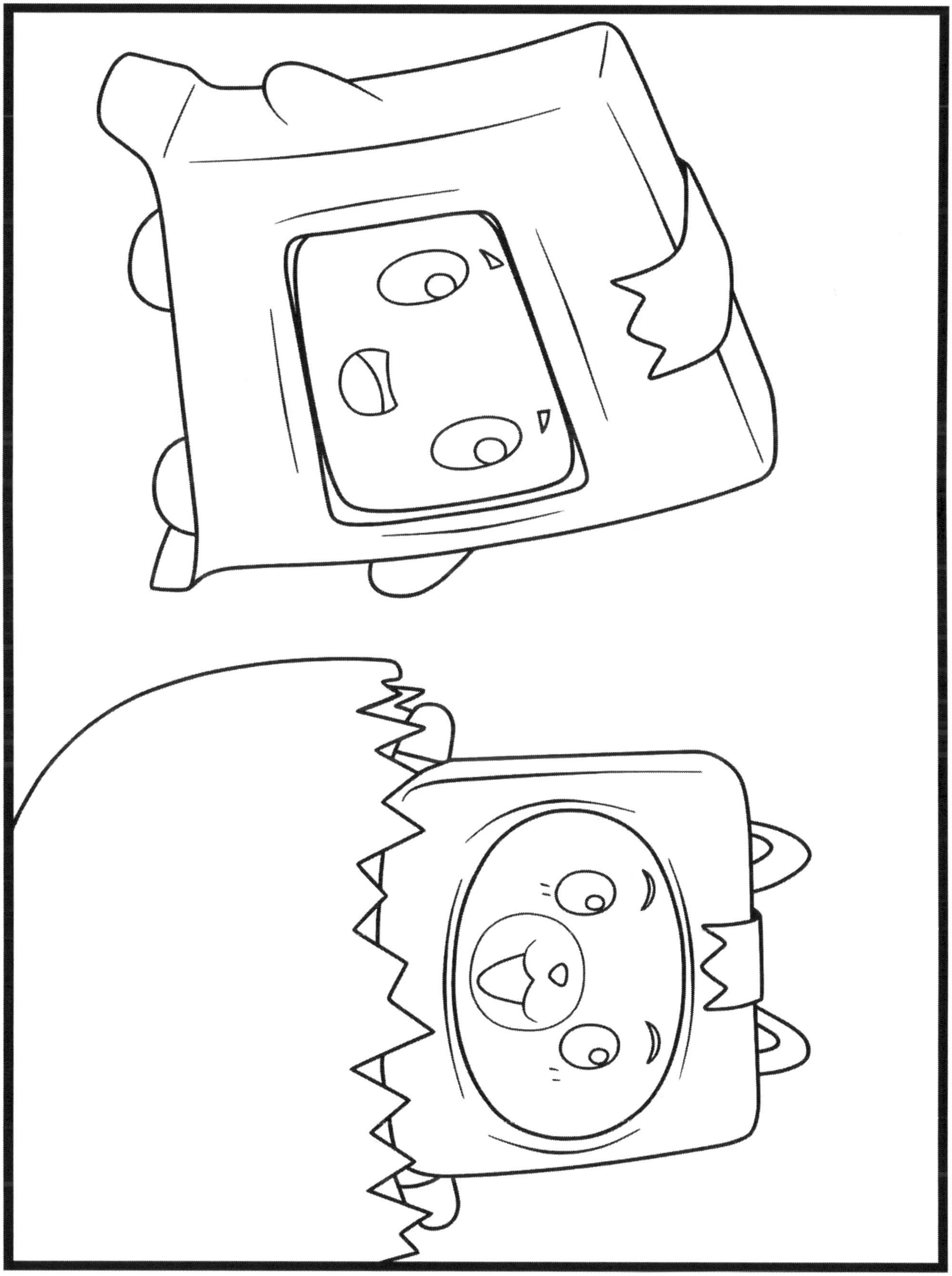

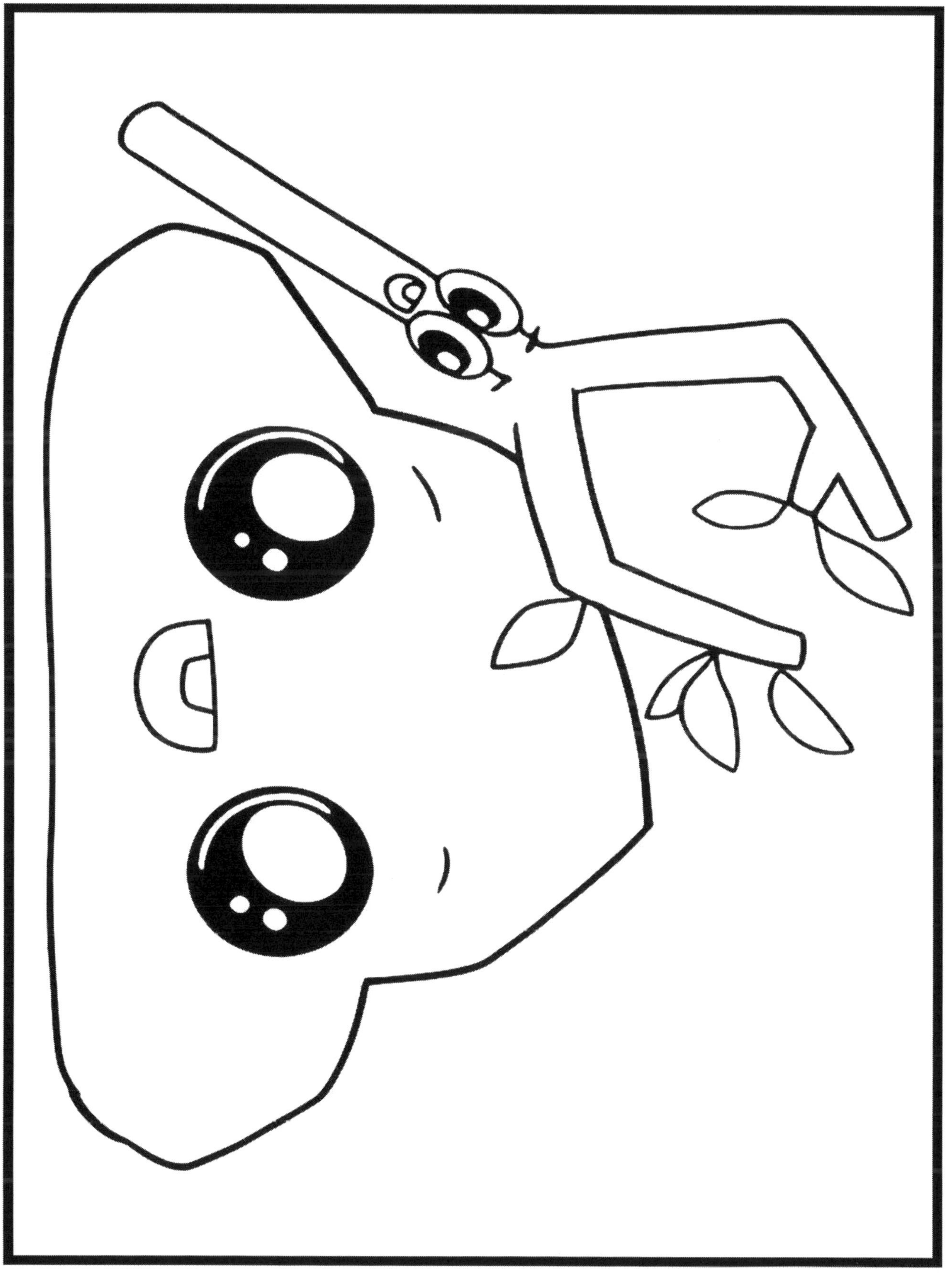

LANKYBOT

F
A+

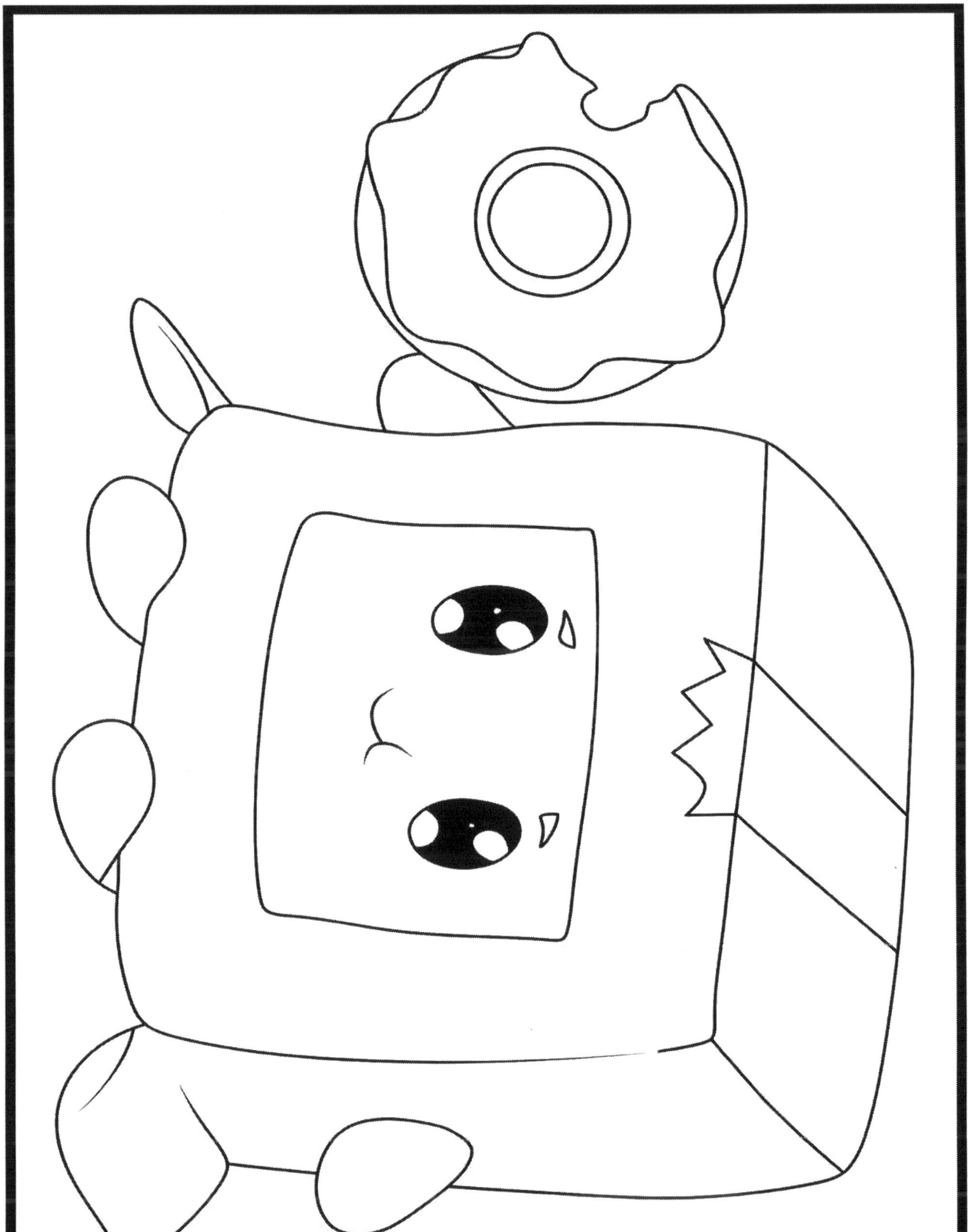

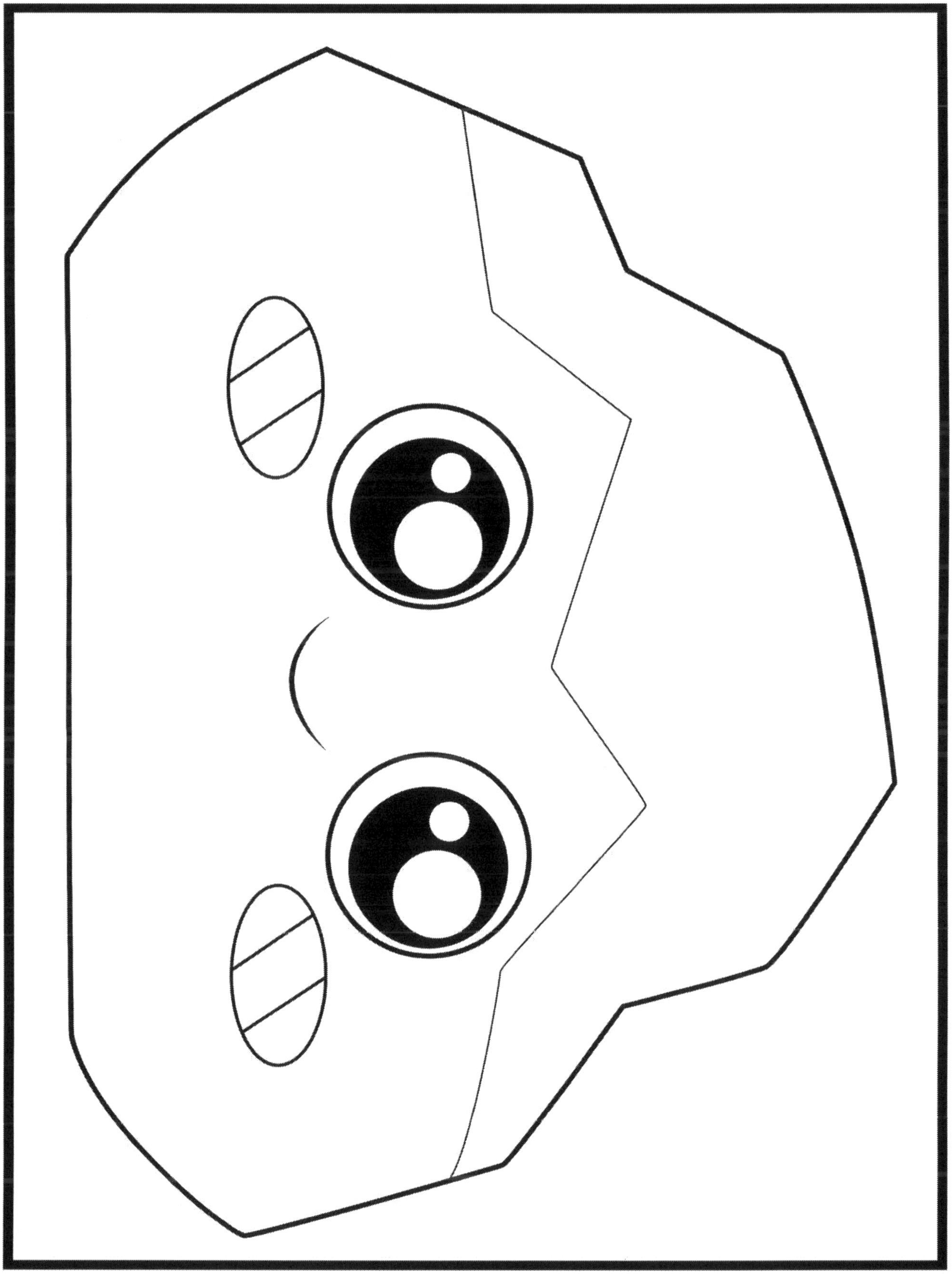

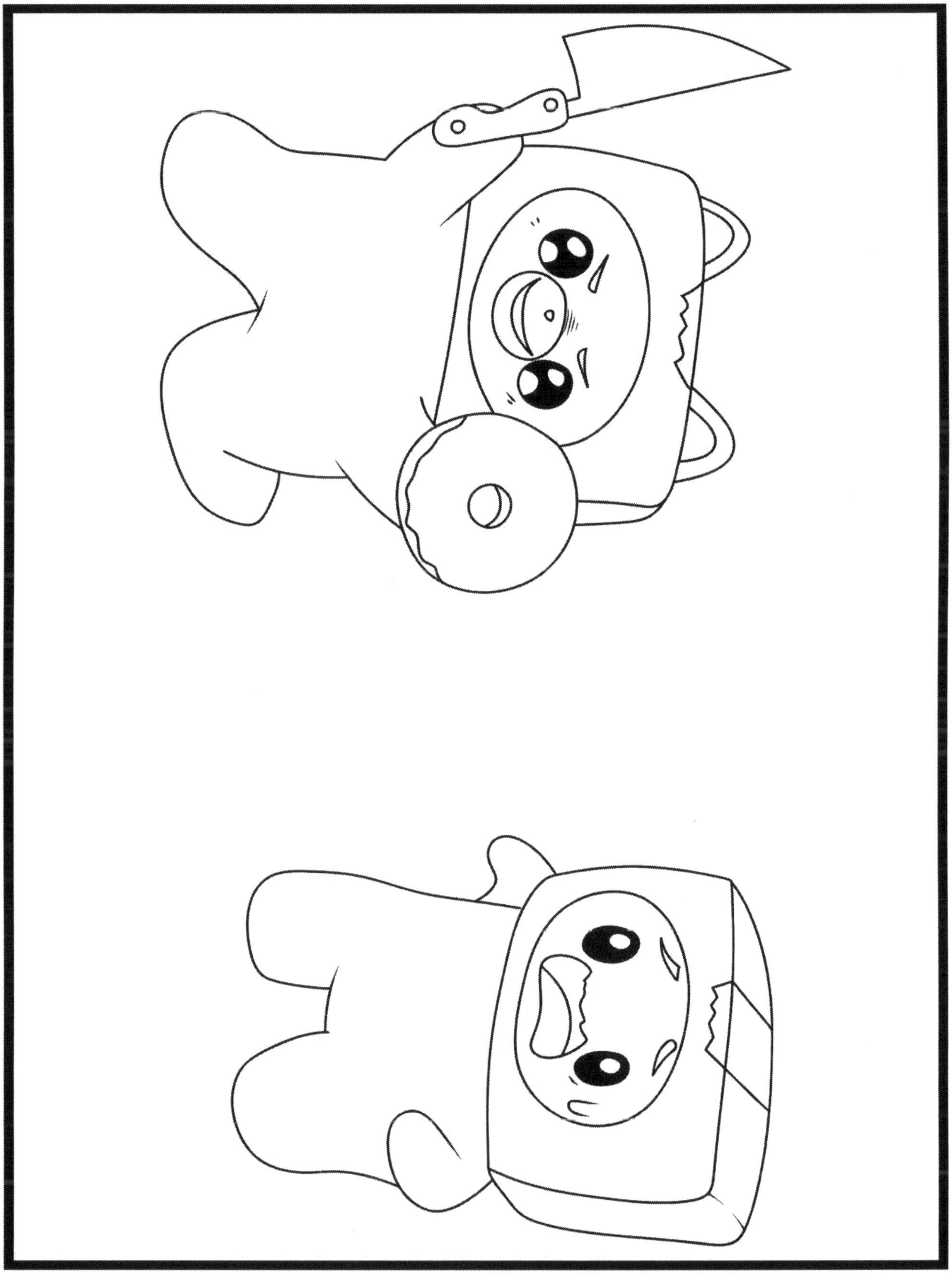

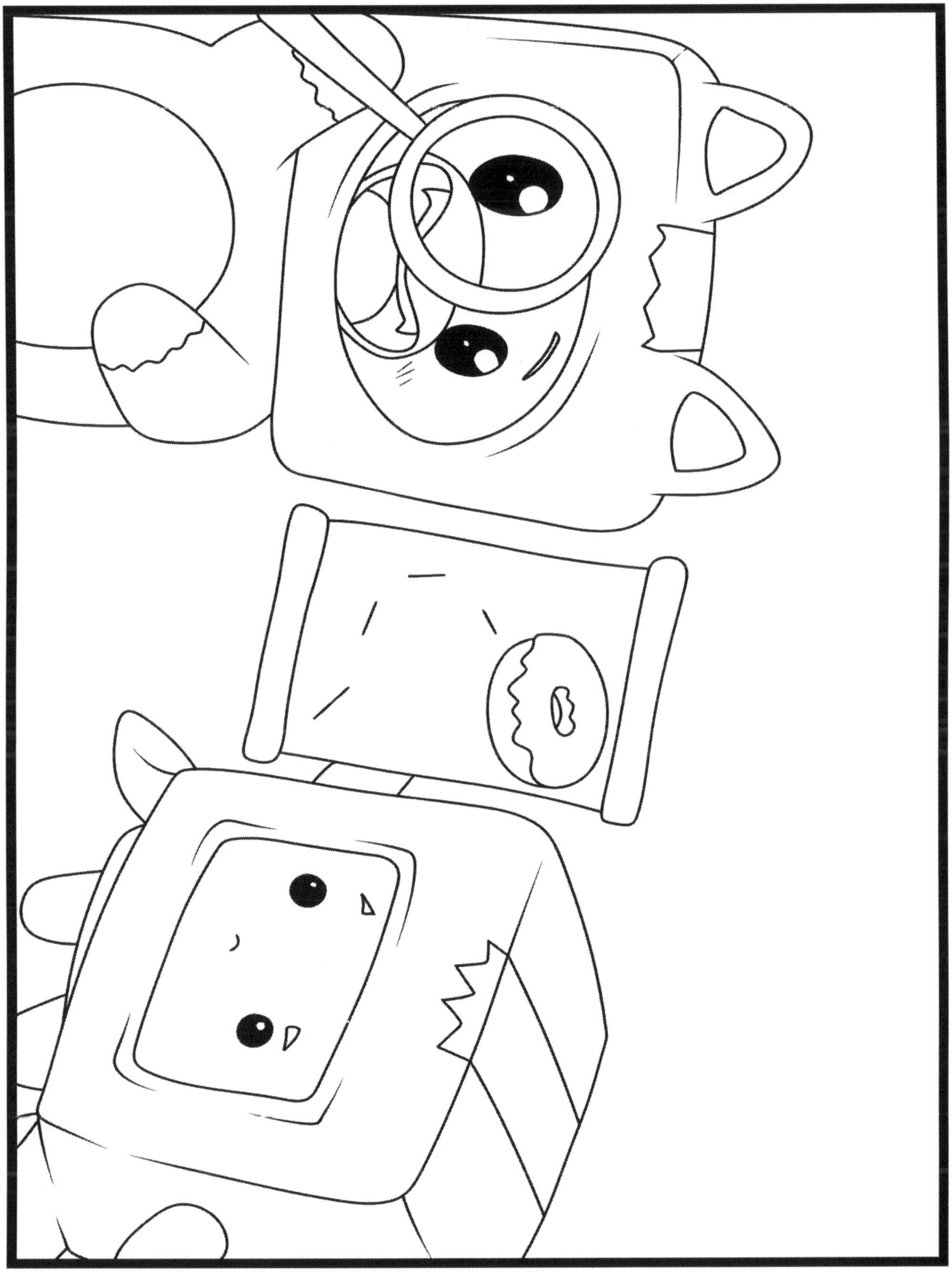

Made in the USA
Columbia, SC
22 November 2024

47247512R00057